THE
2008
GRIFFIN
POETRY
PRIZE
ANTHOLOGY

The 2008 Griffin Poetry Prize Anthology

A SELECTION OF THE SHORTLIST

Edited by GEORGE BOWERING

ANANSI

Published in 2008 by
House of Anansi Press Inc.
110 Spadina Avenue, Suite 801
Toronto, ON, M5V 2K4
Tel. 416-363-4343
Fax 416-363-1017
www.anansi.ca

Distributed in Canada by
HarperCollins Canada Ltd.
1995 Markham Road
Scarborough, ON, M1B 5M8
Toll free tel. 1-800-387-0117

Distributed in the United States by
Publishers Group West
1700 Fourth Street
Berkeley, CA 94710
Toll free tel. 1-800-788-3123

The Griffin Trust and "POETRY" logos used with permission.
Pages 99–100 constitute a continuation of this copyright page.

12 11 10 09 08   1 2 3 4 5

Library and Archives Canada Cataloguing in Publication Data

The 2008 Griffin poetry prize anthology : a selection of the shortlist / edited by George Bowering.

ISBN: 978-0-88784-789-9

1. English poetry — 21st century. 2. Canadian poetry (English) — 21st century.
I. Bowering, George, 1935–

PS8293.1.T96 2008   821'.9208   C2007-907358-1

Library of Congress Control Number: 2007908574

Cover design: Key Gordon Communications
Cover art: Silvia Safdie
Text design and layout: Ingrid Paulson

 Canada Council   Conseil des Arts
for the Arts   du Canada

 ONTARIO ARTS COUNCIL
CONSEIL DES ARTS DE L'ONTARIO

*We acknowledge for their financial support of our publishing program
the Canada Council for the Arts, the Ontario Arts Council, and the Government of Canada
through the Book Publishing Industry Development Program (BPIDP).*

Printed and bound in Canada

CONTENTS

CANADIAN FINALISTS

PREFACE

O for ten years, that I may overwhelm
Myself in poesy

So yearned John Keats in "Sleep and Poetry." Well, for a few
months my fellow adjudicators and I have been getting more
poetry than sleep. James Lasdun, Pura López-Colomé, and I have
certainly learned about being overwhelmed in the stuff. Sure, it
really seemed like Christmas morning when the mailman came
down the chimney with a dozen cartons of books, but we learned
quickly to go on about the work, the duty, and so on. For the most
part, it was a pleasant duty. Every hour spent in the company of
poetry's language meant an hour away from the degrading or
manipulating aims of those who seek to use words as tools and to
use those tools to make us fretful.

So we toiled, James and Pura and I, looking for seven books of
poetry to compose two shortlists for the amazingly generous
prizes given by Mr. and Mrs. Griffin to purveyors of Keats's art.
Each of us assembled longer shortlists, and when Ruth Smith, the
patient and redoubtable manager of the Griffin Trust brought us
together in a conference call — Lo! — our lists were a little similar
and bafflingly diverse. Speaking from New York State, Mexico,
British Columbia, and Scotland, we politely compared notes and
proposed ententes and agreed on a few more weeks of rereading.
When we talked again we came to fashion a shortlist that none of
us would have proposed alone. We were all happy and sad. But we

knew that poetry itself was going to stand in the winner's light. That was Scott Griffin's plan all along.

It is difficult
to get the news from poems
yet men die miserably every day
for lack
of what is found there.

So said William Carlos Williams in "Asphodel, that Greeny Flower." Late in his life he was recalling Ezra Pound's statement that poetry is news that stays news. I think that we who are poets are poets because we are readers, because we have always *wanted* to be readers. We want to read the world we find ourselves in. If this reading will not save our lives or save them from misery, it will help us in the search that creation set us — to figure it out. It is that search that brings us an always surprising if familiar reward we tend to call love. As the man said, it is form that we love when the words come together; it's wisdom we glimpse when understanding and love come together. Poetry is not the only thing that will help that happen, but it is the one that is closest to the language we hear in our heads.

If I am getting a little satin here, I apologize. I mean to say that poetry has been around as long as human beings have. It is tempting to say that poetry is what *made* us human out of whatever we were. It is everywhere, in every family, up every river. James and Pura and I should not have been surprised to see hundreds and hundreds of poetry books materialize on our tables and floors on Christmas morning. And what a way to celebrate the new year!

George Bowering
Vancouver, B.C., April 2008

INTERNATIONAL
FINALISTS

JOHN ASHBERY

Notes from the Air: Selected Later Poems

The pleasure of reading John Ashbery's poetry defies explanation. The YOU the author makes reference to is ME, the *transcription* being rendered, paradoxically, by a poet who eschews autobiography; thus the I as well as the YOU names the reader. Ashbery's is one of the best and most intense poetry productions of the twentieth century. Its famous difficulty does not repel: it invites. It offers a "site of survival," a real mirror for human beings today, providing a place of honour and dignity for the very personal and secret hidden in everyone. His poems reach the private part of each individual. No wonder he has declared in interviews that he's "like everybody else"— the body breathing inside the poem is as much himself as ourselves. But the person who knows how to observe and therefore how to be unique is John Ashbery, ungraspable, inexplicable, and as mysterious as the Delphic oracle.

Someone You Have Seen Before

It was a night for listening to Corelli, Geminiani
Or Manfredini. The tables had been set with beautiful white cloths
And bouquets of flowers. Outside the big glass windows
The rain drilled mercilessly into the rock garden, which made light
Of the whole thing. Both business and entertainment waited
With parted lips, because so much new way of being
With one's emotion and keeping track of it at the same time
Had been silently expressed. Even the waiters were happy.

It was an example of how much one can grow lustily
Without fracturing the shell of coziness that surrounds us,
And all things as well. "We spend so much time
Trying to convince ourselves we're happy that we don't recognize
The real thing when it comes along," the Disney official said.
He's got a point, you must admit. If we followed nature
More closely we'd realize that, I mean really getting your face pressed
Into the muck and indecision of it. Then it's as if
We grew out of our happiness, not the other way round, as is
Commonly supposed. We're the characters in its novel,
And anybody who doubts that need only look out of the window
Past his or her own reflection, to the bright, patterned,
Timeless unofficial truth hanging around out there,
Waiting for the signal to be galvanized into a crowd scene,
Joyful or threatening, it doesn't matter, so long as we know
It's inside, here with us.

But people do change in life,
As well as in fiction. And what happens then? Is it because we think
    nobody's
Listening that one day it comes, the urge to delete yourself,
"Take yourself out," as they say? As though this could matter
Even to the concerned ones who crowd around,

Expressions of lightness and peace on their faces,
In which you play no part perhaps, but even so
Their happiness is for you, it's your birthday, and even
When the balloons and fudge get tangled with extraneous
Good wishes from everywhere, it is, I believe, made to order
For your questioning stance and that impression
Left on the inside of your pleasure by some bivalve
With which you have been identified. Sure,
Nothing is ever perfect enough, but that's part of how it fits
The mixed bag
Of leftover character traits that used to be part of you
Before the change was performed
And of all those acquaintances bursting with vigor and
Humor, as though they wanted to call you down
Into closeness, not for being close, or snug, or whatever,
But because they believe you were made to fit this unique
And valuable situation whose lid is rising, totally
Into the morning-glory-colored future. Remember, don't throw away
The quadrant of unused situations just because they're here:
They may not always be, and you haven't finished looking
Through them all yet. So much that happens happens in small ways
That someone was going to get around to tabulate, and then never did,
Yet it all bespeaks freshness, clarity and an even motor drive
To coax us out of sleep and start us wondering what the new round
Of impressions and salutations is going to leave in its wake
This time. And the form, the precepts, are yours to dispose of as you will,
As the ocean makes grasses, and in doing so refurbishes a lighthouse
On a distant hill, or else lets the whole picture slip into foam.

Token Resistance

As one turns to one in a dream
smiling like a bell that has just
stopped tolling, holds out a book,
and speaks: "All the vulgarity

of time, from the Stone Age
to our present, with its noodle parlors
and token resistance, is as a life
to the life that is given you. Wear it,"

so must one descend from checkered heights
that are our friends, needlessly
rehearsing what we will say
as a common light bathes us,

a common fiction reverberates as we pass
to the celebration. Originally
we weren't going to leave home. But made bold
somehow by the rain we put our best foot forward.

Now it's years after that. It
isn't possible to be young anymore.
Yet the tree treats me like a brute friend;
my own shoes have scarred the walk I've taken.

He was a soldier or a Shaker. At least he was doing *something*,
going somewhere. Often, in the evenings, he'd rant about Mark Twain,
how that wasn't his real name, and was he hiding something?
If so, then why call himself a humorist?
We began to tire of his ravings, but (as so often happens)
it was just at that point that a salient character trait
revealed itself, or rather, manifested itself within him.
It was one of those goofy days in August
when all men (and some women) dream of chocolate sodas.
He confessed he'd had one for lunch,
then took us out to the street to show us the whir and dazzle
of living in some other city, where so much that is different goes on.
I guess he was inspired by Lahore. Said it came to him
in his dreams every night. And little by little
we felt ourselves being transported there. Not that we wanted
to be there, far from that. But we were either too timid
or unaware to urge him otherwise. Then he mentioned Timbuktu.
Said he'd actually been there, that the sidewalks were pink
and the huts made of mother-of-pearl, not mud, as is commonly
supposed. Said he'd had the best venison and apple tart
in his life there.
                    Well, we were accompanying him in the daze
that usually surrounded him, when we began to think about ourselves:
When *was* the last time we had done so? And the stranger shifted shape
again (he was now wearing a Zouave's culottes), and asked us
would we want to *live* in Djibouti, or Providence, or Lyon, now that
we'd seen them, and we chorused (like frogs), Oh no, we
want to live in New York, not that the other places aren't as splendid
and interesting as you say. It's just that New York
feels more like home to us. It's ugly, it's dirty, the people are rude

(kind and rude), and every surface has a fine film of filth
on it that behooves slobs like us, and will in time turn to diamonds,
just like the mother-of-pearl shacks in Timbuktu. And he said,
You know I was wrong about Mark Twain. It was his real name,
and he was a humorist, a genuine American humorist for the ages.

Memories of Imperialism

Dewey took Manila
and soon after invented the decimal system
that keeps libraries from collapsing even unto this day.
A lot of mothers immediately started naming their male offspring "Dewey,"
which made him queasy. He was already having second thoughts about
     imperialism.
In his dreams he saw library books with milky numbers
on their spines floating in Manila Bay.
Soon even words like "vanilla" or "mantilla" would cause him to vomit.
The sight of a manila envelope precipitated him
into his study, where all day, with the blinds drawn,
he would press fingers against temples, muttering "What have I done?"
all the while. Then, gradually, he began feeling a bit better.
The world hadn't ended. He'd go for walks in his old neighborhood,
marveling at the changes there, or at the lack of them. "If one is
to go down in history, it is better to do so for two things
rather than one," he would stammer, none too meaningfully.

One day his wife took him aside
in her boudoir, pulling the black lace mantilla from her head
and across her bare breasts until his head was entangled in it.
"Honey, what am I supposed to say?" "Say nothing, you big boob.
Just be glad you got away with it and are famous." "Speaking of
boobs..." "Now you're getting the idea. Go file those books
on those shelves over there. Come back only when you're finished."

To this day schoolchildren wonder about his latter career
as a happy pedant, always nice with children, thoughtful
toward their parents. He wore a gray ceramic suit
walking his dog, a "bouledogue," he would point out.
People would peer at him from behind shutters, watchfully,
hoping no new calamities would break out, or indeed
that nothing more would happen, ever, that history had ended.
Yet it hadn't, as the admiral himself
would have been the first to acknowledge.

The New Higher

You meant more than life to me. I lived through
you not knowing, not knowing I was living.
I learned that you called for me. I came to where
you were living, up a stair. There was no one there.
No one to appreciate me. The legality of it
upset a chair. Many times to celebrate
we were called together and where
we had been there was nothing there,
nothing that is anywhere. We passed obliquely,
leaving no stare. When the sun was done muttering,
in an optimistic way, it was time to leave that there.

Blithely passing in and out of where, blushing shyly
at the tag on the overcoat near the window where
the outside crept away, I put aside the there and now.
Now it was time to stumble anew,
blacking out when time came in the window.
There was not much of it left.
I laughed and put my hands shyly
across your eyes. Can you see now?
Yes I can see I am only in the where
where the blossoming stream takes off, under your window.
Go presently you said. Go from my window.
I am half in love with your window I cannot undermine
it, I said.

Interesting People of Newfoundland

Newfoundland is, or was, full of interesting people.
Like Larry, who would make a fool of himself on street corners
for a nickel. There was the Russian who called himself
the Grand Duke, and who was said to be a real duke from somewhere,
and the woman who frequently accompanied him on his rounds.
Doc Hanks, the sawbones, was a real good surgeon
when he wasn't completely drunk, which was most of the time.
When only half drunk he could perform decent cranial surgery.
There was the blind man who never said anything
but produced spectral sounds on a musical saw.

There was Walsh's, with its fancy grocery department.
What a treat when Mother or Father
would take us down there, skidding over slippery snow
and ice, to be rewarded with a rare fig from somewhere.
They had teas from every country you could imagine
and hard little cakes from Scotland, rare sherries
and Madeiras to reward the aunts and uncles who came dancing.
On summer evenings in the eternal light it was a joy
just to be there and think. We took long rides
into the countryside, but were always stopped by some bog or other.
Then it was time to return home, which was OK with everybody,
each of them having discovered he or she could use a little shuteye.

In short there was a higher per capita percentage of interesting people
there than almost anywhere on earth, but the population was small,
which meant not too many interesting people. But for all that
we loved each other and had interesting times
picking each other's brain and drying nets on the wooden docks.
Always some more of us would come along. It is in the place
in the world in complete beauty, as none can gainsay,
I declare, and strong frontiers to collide with.

Worship of the chthonic powers may well happen there
but is seldom in evidence. We loved that too,
as we were a part of all that happened there, the evil and the good
and all the shades in between, happy to pipe up at roll call
or compete in the spelling bees. It was too much of a good thing
but at least it's over now. They are making a pageant out of it,
one of them told me. It's coming to a theater near you.

ELAINE EQUI

Ripple Effect: New and Selected Poems

In a warmly appreciative essay on Frank O'Hara, Elaine Equi gives a description of the poet's distinct way of walking, as recalled by his friend Joe Brainard: "Light and sassy. With a slight bounce and a slight twist. It was a beautiful walk. Confident. 'I don't care' and sometimes 'I know you are looking.'" The words could stand as an accurate description of Equi's own highly distinct poems. They too move with a bounce and twist; they have their own insouciant, confident wit, their own beautifully poised way of looking outward at the world in all its quirky variousness, while at the same time retaining an uncompromised inwardness: the registering of a complex, sophisticated poetic self. Founded on a casual mastery of modernist and post-modernist techniques — montage, free-form improvisation, prose-poem, surreal inventory, found object — her work is at once impeccably avant garde and immensely enjoyable. Her poems don't try to change the world, but as they rifle through it, pausing to think about sleeping pills or sales catalogues or Wang Wei or "a factory made fresh by broken windows," they use their abundant resources of humour, intelligence, and verbal acuity to change the way we, as readers, see the world.

Invocation

Come Inspiration,

sweet as two beautiful hookers
in a dream.

Don't go girls —

even if you don't know a thing
about poetry,

at least help me decide
what to wear.

John Coltrane's Central Park West

Now this is the music
I imagine playing
if I were having an affair
with myself as a married man.

It's the music that would
always remind me
I always have me
in a special way
even if we aren't actually wed.

Found in Translation

I've always liked reading poetry in translation. In fact, I prefer it that way.

Poetry is the sound one language makes when it escapes into another.

Whatever you think you've missed is, as the saying goes, better left to the imagination.

It gives even a mediocre poem an ineffable essence.

Greater involvement on the part of the reader leads to greater enjoyment.

A bad translation, a clumsy one, is especially charming.

The poem is whatever cannot be killed by the translator.

Its will to survive, its willingness to be uprooted and flee its homeland is admirable. I almost want to say virile.

An untranslated poem is too attached to its author. It's too raw.

An untranslatable poem that hordes its meaning, whose borders are too guarded, is better unsaid.

For years, I copied authors from around the world. Then one day it occurred to me, perhaps it's the translator I imitate, not the poet. This idea pleases me and makes me want to write more.

It would be great to learn French in order to read William Carlos Williams.

Translators are the true transcendentalists.

Echo
for Robert Creeley

It's all about
the lag time

between reflections
when Narcissus thinks:

it's my face,

only wetter,
maybe longer,

me but
not entirely —

something missing,
added?

I can't take my eyes
off it

(wait, are those my eyes?)

I Interview Elaine Equi on the Four Elements

Q: What is your favorite element?

A: Definitely air. It's the medium of thought.
    Ethereal. Invisible. And even better than air,
    I love heights. I'm the opposite of someone with
    acrophobia. Space travel sounds appealing.

Q: Which element do you like least?

A: Water. It makes me nervous. You can't walk on it.
    Both my parents are Pisces so perhaps that explains...
    I'm a terrible swimmer.

Q: Being a Leo, do you feel at home with fire?

A: I like light, but not heat. I don't even like hot
    sauce. I could never see myself as a pyromaniac.

Q: Which brings us to earth, what associations do you
    have with it?

A: The earth has always supported me in all my
    endeavors. I trust it.

Prescription

Take Herrick
for melancholy

Niedecker
for clarity

O'Hara
for nerve

Sometimes I Get Distracted
for Philip Whalen

Throwing a ball

like a bridge
over an old wound

like a cape
thrown chivalrously
over incoherent muck.

Catching it
is easy.

"Now toss it back,"

says the Zen monk
standing in his garden
centuries away.

The Banal

Even with its shitload of artifacts, the everyday
is radiant, while the banal is opaque and often
obscure. I prefer the latter, with its murky
agate, mushroom, ochre background music —
its corridor of lurk. One hardly knows where
one stands with/in the banal. Walls come
together with hardly a seam. Wherever we are, we
feel we have always been. Poe, for all his special
effects, is rather banal in his approach to the
supernatural, i.e. overly familiar. Against the
inarticulate velvet of this mood, one grasps at
the everyday for relief. Thus any object can
bring us back with the fast-acting power of
aspirin. Any object shines.

Dolor

Dolor — sadness kept as a powder in small jars
sometimes distinguished by a Greek label
and scented with vanilla.
As in the sentence:
he drave her away and took out his jar of dolor.

Friable — easily crumbled:
the dolor was friable to a point.

Depute — appoint to do one's work:
when the dolor was missing, strangers were deputed
to recover it.

CLAYTON ESHLEMAN
(translator)

CÉSAR VALLEJO

The Complete Poetry: A Bilingual Edition

When Mario Vargas Llosa refers to the work of Clayton Eshleman as a sort of heroic enterprise, he is hitting the target — life given as an act of love. Here are more than five decades of perseverance, polishing and devotion to translation of someone who has been called inexplicable. And if we have untranslatability, we have what would seem to be an impossible task. Eshleman's versions deserve not only praise, but many readers. Most important, he has followed Cid Corman's teachings: respect for the original, along with absolute awareness of the fact that one is creating *something else*. The result has been the wonderfully rendered complete work of a very complex poet in terms of imagination and style, of multilayered registers — a poet who aspires to wholeness of expression, the world and his perception as the same thing, full of ambivalence and contradiction, a poet who deep down didn't want to be translated, having enormous doubts as to the capacity even of one's own language to confront sadness and human grief. Eshleman has opened, as have few others, a window to another life, a new one, not necessarily his nor Vallejo's.

Altarpiece

I tell myself: at last I have escaped the noise;
no one sees me on my way to the sacred nave.
Tall shades attend,
and Darío who passes with lyre in mourning.

With innumerable steps the gentle Muse emerges,
and my eyes go to her, like chicks to corn.
Ethereal tulles and sleeping titmice harass her,
while the blackbird of life dreams in her hand.

My God, you are merciful, for you have bestowed this nave
where these blue sorcerers perform their duties.
Darío of celestial Americas! They are so much
like you! And from your braids they make their hair shirts.

Like souls seeking burials of absurd gold,
these wayward archpriests of the heart,
probe deeper, and appear...and, addressing us from afar,
bewail the monotonous suicide of God!

Januneid

My father can hardly,
in the bird-borne morning, get
his seventy-eight years, his seventy-eight
winter branches, out into the sunlight.
The Santiago graveyard, anointed
with Happy New Year, is in view.
How many times his footsteps have cut over toward it,
then returned from some humble burial.

Today it's a long time since my father went out!
A hubbub of kids breaks up.

Other times he would talk to my mother
about city life, politics;
today, supported by his distinguished cane
(which sounded better during his years in office),
my father is unknown, frail,
my father is a vesper.
He carries, brings, absentmindedly, relics, things,
memories, suggestions.
The placid morning accompanies him
with its white Sister of Charity wings.

This is an eternal day, an ingenuous, childlike,
choral, prayerful day;
time is crowned with doves
and the future is filled with
caravans of immortal roses.
Father, yet everything is still awakening;
it is January that sings, it is your love

that keeps resonating in Eternity.
You will laugh with your little ones,
and there will be a triumphant racket in the Void.

    It will still be New Year. There will be empanadas;
and I will be hungry, when Mass is rung
in the pious bell tower by
the kind melic blind man with whom
my fresh schoolboy syllables, my rotund
innocence, chatted.
And when the morning full of grace,
from its breasts of time,
which are two renunciations, two advances of love
which stretch out and plead for infinity, eternal life,
sings, and lets fly plural Words,
tatters of your being,
at the edge of its white
Sister of Charity wings, oh! my father!

The moment the tennis player masterfully serves
his bullet, a totally animal innocence possesses him;
the moment
the philosopher surprises a new truth,
he is an absolute beast.
Anatole France affirmed
that religious feeling
is the function of a special organ in the human body,
until now unrecognized and one could
also say, then,
that the exact moment when such an organ
fully functions
the believer is so clear of malice,
he could almost be considered a vegetable.
Oh soul! Oh thought! Oh Marx! Oh Feuerbach!

The Footfalls of a Great Criminal

When they turned off the lights, I felt like laughing. Things renewed their labors in the dark, at the point where they had been stopped; in a face, the eyes lowered to the nasal shells and took an inventory of certain missing optical powers, retrieving them one by one; a naval scale imperiously summoned the scales of a fish; three parallel raindrops halted at the height of a lintel, awaiting another drop that doesn't know why it has been delayed; the policeman on the corner blew his nose noisily, emphasizing in particular his left nostril; the highest and the lowest steps of a spiral staircase began to make signs to each other that alluded to the last passerby to climb them. Things, in the dark, renewed their labors, animated by an uninhibited happiness, conducting themselves like people at a great ceremonial banquet, where the lights went out and all remained in the dark.

When they turned off the light, a better distribution of boundaries and frames was carried out around the world. Each rhythm was its own music; each needle of a scale moved as little as a destiny could move, that is to say, until nearly acquiring an absolute presence. In general, a delightful game was created between things, one of liberation and justice. I watched them and grew content, since in myself as well the grace of the numeral dark curvetted.

I don't know who let there be light again. The world began to crouch once more in its shabby pelts: the yellow one of Sunday, the ashen one of Monday, the humid one of Tuesday, the judicious one of Wednesday, sharkskin for Thursday, a sad one for Friday, a tattered one for Saturday. Thus the world reappeared, quiet, sleeping, or pretending to sleep. A hair-raising spider, with three broken legs, emerged from Saturday's sleeve.

Farewell Remembering a Good-Bye

At the end, in the end, at last,
I turn, I've returned and I'm finished and moan to you, giving you
the key, my hat, this brief letter for everyone.
At the end of the key is the metal where we learned
to ungild the gold, and there is, in the end
of my hat, this poor brain badly combed,
and, a last glass of smoke, on its dramatic role,
this practical dream of the soul rests.

Good-bye, brother Saint Peters,
Heraclituses, Erasmuses, Spinozas!
Good-bye, sad Bolshevik bishops!
Good-bye, governers in turmoil!
Good-bye, wine that's in water like wine!
Good-bye, alcohol that's in the rain!

Good-bye, likewise, I say to myself,
good-bye, formal flight of milligrams!
Likewise good-bye, in an identical way,
cold of the cold and the cold of warmth!
At the end, in the end, at last, logic,
the boundaries of fire,
the farewell remembering that good-bye.

A man walks by with a baguette on his shoulder
Am I going to write, after that, about my double?

Another sits, scratches, extracts a louse from his armpit, kills it
How dare one speak about psychoanalysis?

Another has entered my chest with a stick in hand
To talk then about Socrates with the doctor?

A cripple passes by holding a child's hand
After that I'm going to read André Breton?

Another trembles from cold, coughs, spits blood
Will it ever be possible to allude to the deep Self?

Another searches in the muck for bones, rinds
How to write, after that, about the infinite?

A bricklayer falls from a roof, dies and no longer eats lunch
To innovate, then, the trope, the metaphor?

A merchant cheats a customer out of a gram
To speak, after that, about the fourth dimension?

A banker falsifies his balance sheet
With what face to cry in the theater?

An outcast sleeps with his foot behind his back
To speak, after that, to anyone about Picasso?

Someone goes to a burial sobbing
How then become a member of the Academy?

Someone cleans a rifle in his kitchen
How dare one speak about the beyond?

Someone passes by counting with his fingers
How speak of the non-self without screaming?

In short, I have nothing with which to express my life, except my death.

And, after everything, at the end of graded nature and of the sparrow in bloc, I sleep, hand in hand with my shadow.

And, upon descending from the venerable act and from the other moan, I repose thinking about the inexorable march of time.

Why the rope, then, if air is so simple? What is the chain for, if iron exists on its own?

César Vallejo, the accent with which you love, the language with which you write, the light wind with which you hear, only know of you through your throat.

César Vallejo, prostrate yourself, therefore, with vague pride, with a nuptial bed of ornamental asps and hexagonal echoes.

Return to the corporeal honeycomb, to beauty; aromatize the blossomed corks, close both grottoes to the enraged anthropoid; mend, finally, your unpleasant stag; feel sorry for yourself.

For there is nothing denser than the hate in a passive voice, no stingier udder than love!

For I'm no longer able to walk, except on two harps!

For you no longer know me, unless instrumentally, longwindedly, I follow you!

For I no longer issue worms, but briefs!

For I now implicate you so much, you almost become sharp!

For I now carry some timid vegetables and others that are fierce!

So the affection that ruptures at night in my bronchia, was brought during the day by occult deans and, if I wake up pale, it's because of my work: and, if I go to sleep red, because of my worker. This explains, equally, this weariness of mine and these spoils, my famous uncles. This explains, finally, this tear that I toast to the happiness of men.

César Vallejo, it's hard
to believe that your relatives are so late,
knowing that I walk a captive,
knowing that you lie free!
Flashy and rotten luck!
César Vallejo, I hate you with tenderness!

Spain, Take This Cup From Me

Children of the world,
if Spain falls — I mean, it's just a thought —
if her forearm
falls downward from the sky seized,
in a halter, by two terrestrial plates;
children, what an age of concave temples!
how early in the sun what I was telling you!
how quickly in your chest the ancient noise!
how old your 2 in the notebook!

Children of the world, mother
Spain is with her belly on her back;
our teacher is with her ferules,
she appears as mother and teacher,
cross and wood, because she gave you height,
vertigo and division and addition, children;
she is with herself, legal parents!

If she falls — I mean, it's just a thought — if Spain
falls, from the earth downward,
children, how you will stop growing!
how the year will punish the month!
how you will never have more than ten teeth,
how the diphthong will remain in downstroke, the gold star in tears!
How the little lamb will stay
tied by its leg to the great inkwell!
How you'll descend the steps of the alphabet
to the letter in which pain was born!

Children,
sons of fighters, meanwhile,
lower your voice, for right at this moment Spain is distributing
her energy among the animal kingdom,
little flowers, comets, and men.
Lower your voice, for she
shudders convulsively, not knowing
what to do, and she has in her hand
the talking skull, chattering away,
the skull, the one with a braid,
the skull, the one with life!

Lower your voice, I tell you;
lower your voice, the song of the syllables, the wail
of matter and the faint murmur of the pyramids, and even
that of your temples which walk with two stones!
Lower your breathing, and if
the forearm comes down,
if the ferules sound, if it is night,
if the sky fits between two terrestrial limbos,
if there is noise in the creaking of doors,
if I am late,
if you do not see anyone, if the blunt pencils
frighten you, if mother
Spain falls — I mean, it's just a thought —
go out, children of the world, go look for her!...

DAVID HARSENT

Selected Poems 1969–2005

The four decades' worth of work spanned by David Harsent's *Selected Poems* reveal a writer of enormous accomplishment in whom a constant, restless investigation of new forms, new subjects, new ways of putting together a poem or sequence of poems, is underpinned by a remarkably consistent and powerful poetic sensibility. You know instantly when you are in a David Harsent poem: the vivid landscapes where the weather shifts as rapidly between inner and outer as it does between bright and menacing; the haunting psychological situations that give you a novel's worth of drama in a few lines; the dense imagery continually opening up the narratives to new levels of suggestion and implication; the controlled riot of language; the intense, fluid musicality. Like the elusive figure of the hare that slips in and out of these poems — a motif borrowed in part from Egyptian writing where it formed the hieroglyph for the auxiliary verb "to be" — the ultimate quarry of these poems, whether pursued through marriage or war or some more indefinite terrain, is nothing less than existence itself: what it feels like to be alive, human, and of this world.

Fylfot

She slept like that
whenever she slept deeply,
one hand here, the other

here, knees tucked up so:
the action of someone rising to a high
hurdle, or going at a slope

where a fall of snow
lies over yesterday's fall
with a night of ice between.

The skyline carried a yellow
and mauve meniscus. Just
past dawn the story said

and, yes,
the troopers had risen in darkness
minutes before,

swearing at everything.
The only warmth
was the smell of bacon and wood-

smoke and dung and leathers.
She could hear
noises beneath the wind: talk, mostly,

and horses,
but when she looked down
to the combe, there was nothing

to see but an officer naked
in front of his tent, arse-out
for a needle-bath.

The deserter arrived like a drunk
in the arms of friends, not much
more than a child himself,

his own child dead,
his wife out of her wits.
They'd picked him up

before he was half way home
the story said and that was right,
more or less; he'd travelled

south to Wistman's Wood, riding
the captain's grey,
then east towards Haytor.

She thumbed up
a jot of blood, crusted
with snow and let it melt

in the cup of her hand.
It might have been from her own
bitten lip; more likely from the raw

bandana he wore
where the halter had been laced.
Two men shook out

bales of hay along the picket line;
the farrier turned his back and pulled
a hoof to his apron;

the cook washed pots in the snow.
The rest of them
made a square, and soon

the Chaplain led them in 'Life
is dark without Thee'
and they drew him up

on to the wheel, working
easily, and broke him to that self-
same shape: fylfot.

The Good Companion

Laid-up with all about me
a man could want: a stack of the cross-
hatched notebooks I always use,
a Stabilo pen,
a brand-new thriller that famously stole its plot
from *The Spanish Tragedy*, vodka,

a pineapple tub
of ice to sap (a little) the bright
fever that loosened my teeth, so I half-expected
to see them drop to the quilt
like sticky Chiclets,
laid-up like that, alone

you might say, but well provided for,
I felt a sleep coming on, so thick
I might have been sleeved in darkness; and next
fell into a dream quicker
than my eyes could close: in fact
I'd already declared for Bel-imperia

and was just getting down
past the damp in the crook of her knee
to those salty, pink petals
of crêpe-de-chine,
when a voice I recognised
had me up and out of there and back to my bed —

a hot, synaptic *zip*
that almost made me believe I'd woken up
until I saw the tattoo:
a letter to every finger neatly between

the knuckle joints,
as he collared the bottle and turned

a page or two of my notebooks. 'Just here:
is this *lorel* or *Lorelei*?'— each syllable sharp
as the detonations in ice
when you pour on vodka —'It's plain
what's fretting you, but look,
you'll know it sure enough

when someone you claim to recognise climbs up
out of your bones
and legs it for the door
without so much as a kiss-
my-arse-goodbye (on a darkening day of "rain
moving in from the west") or even a shred of song.'

Marriage xv

Now rise from the bath, your hair caught up with a peg.
The water peels back from your breasts like the film from
    a cooking egg.
You cleanly cleave your arse as you lift one leg

to the edge of the tub and start to work the towel
from ankle to thigh, then into the damson bevel
of your crotch, after which you sit, heel to knee,

on a raffia chair, your quim guerning to a scowl
as you slip your foot into the foot
of your stocking. Next, it's your face coming free

of the summer dress, as you greet
yourself in the mirror. Here's how it goes after that:
    foundation, powder, eye-
shadow, blusher, mascara,

lipstick pressed to a tissue...that perfectly mute
syllable of love (love, or it could be hate)
that I pick up and pocket to re-read later.

The same summer dress you loosened and dropped with a
    clatter
of tiny buttons on tile as I backed you up to the table,
our first night under this roof, and you The Biddable

Spouse, slipping your foot out of the foot
of your stocking...The same table
you cover with a red checkered cloth, setting the bread,
    the butter,

the plum preserve, and the best we have of china.
Ur-wife. Wife of wives.
I'm close enough for ambush as you pass with your box
    of knives.

Chinese Whispers

They told us about the boy who disappeared
when the convoy went through. Search
as they might there was no sign until word
was sent of 'residue' between the wheel and the wheel-arch.

. . .

News arrived of the women who went mad,
who kicked-in the windows of every billet,
who ran shrieking through the Street of Locks, who shed
their semmits and stays to dance a *carcan* in the market.

. . .

This one's got legs: the man who went down to the river
under fire, searching among that day's dead for his only
    brother,
turning the bodies, one by one, to discover
his wife, son, uncles, sister, father, mother.

. . .

The Surgeon General, they say it was, who went back
to drink the last of his Roffignac, to sit in a dry bath
and open a vein: a man, for sure, on the right track.
One for the road. One for the primrose path.

. . .

Hardly a day goes by but someone boasts
of having been there when those men downed weapons
with barely a word, and walked through their own lines,
later reported as slips of the tongue, or ghosts.

. . .

How's this for a tale of slaughter:
a man who slew his herd, then drew a hood
over the trembling head of each blonde daughter
and shot them where they stood?

. . .

Word of mouth has a gut-shot man walk all of ten
miles from the front to his own front door, lift the latch,
find them dead, dig seven graves, fire the thatch,
fill his bottle, sling his gun, walk back again.

. . .

Here's one about the raw recruit who crawled out from
    beneath
the corpses of his comrades, like a dinner guest
emerging from a bun-fight scrum, to charge the machine-
    gun nest
armed with only a shovel, with only a trowel, with only
    a toothpick, with only his teeth.

Arena

Not everything dead is buried in that place
of rapid shadows. They're all in place, some head-

to-tail or arse-up, some cheek-by-jowl or face
to face (whether or not they were married), some in place

of others who say there's nothing to be said
and turn the earth at night and know their place.

The markers are blank, since everything's taken as read
in a place like that. Not everything buried is dead.

CANADIAN FINALISTS

ROBIN BLASER

The Holy Forest: Collected Poems of Robin Blaser

There is an irony in the presumption that the universe contains the "collected" poems of Robin Blaser. Within the five hundred pages of *The Holy Forest* moves a lifetime's thought such as we are not used to or prepared for. Whitman was not fooling when he said that a poet, an extraordinary poet, can himself be a cosmos. But as sidereal as Blaser's lines become, we never forget that the purpose is human living every day inside what is. In a review of an earlier volume with the same title (bravely published in Canada by Coach House Books and later listed by Talonbooks) Brian Fawcett wrote: "His truest poetic instinct is that cosmology is at once humanity's fundamental pursuit — and the source of our most screamingly funny ironies, misapprehensions, and pratfalls." Blaser is solemn enough to approach Dante Alighieri as a "Great Companion," and serious enough to maintain that "the truth is laughter" we might find some afternoon on the darkest pavement.

Luck   Unluck   One Luck

the heart turns inside out
of the mouth and eyes
out of the indeterminate ear
      blue dogs of the hillside   hunt
the skin-play
         of suddenness

the Egyptians did not close the mouth
and the eyes   at the edge of the sun
but opened them   and gave boats

1945   Rosario Jimenez, who at the round
         table   read García Lorca and Homer,
         talks to herself behind the glass door,

1948   Ernst Kantorowicz, who taught the
         young   to think swiftly   an essential
         history
               like Richard's
         robe only he could take off
         divinity alone removes the divinity
         of an empty coat

1945–1965 Jack Spicer, who tore himself up
         in language   'I can't bear it,' I said,
         then studied his peril and task

    19–   the *hound-voice*
                    of earth and sky,
      men, women, and gods   folding
                     inside

the effacement of words   the puns
in ice
                 a laughter
a voice thins on a cigarette   chokes
to a whisper   and sharpens
the edge of the blade
                           who is speaking
I hear the other toss-up

'knowledge is a moth,'   a friend sent
on a postcard   with Michael Snow's
camera of the central region on the front
          there
in the mountains   all by itself and
a singing computer
                           the horizon
first ahead of you   at your edge
then around you   without you

in the motionless light of a mineral
in the white perfume of a magnolia
pink-edged   *on the fleshy*   spotted
and almost black abyss of a poppy
so we have exchanged mutual forgiveness
with the eye of a cat
                           the unknowing
like a fish-hook
                      of fire-flower
eaten petals
                      the eagle is perched
there on the tongue   at the mouth

white flowers unsheathe
                    to resolve language
ahead of it

                         behind the fire
from unknown mouths
the wind rises
where that would not become god

−74

Fortune   Infortune   Fort Une

Suddenly,

I live in a room named East
on the map of the West   at the edge

near the door cedars and alders
mix and tower,
full of ravens   first thing each morning,
whose song is
                a sharpness

we quarrelled so
                    over the genius
of the heart
                whose voice is capable

they come on horseback
in the middle of the night,
two of them,   with a horse for me,
and we ride,   bareback
clinging to the white manes
at the edge of the sea-splash,

burst open,

                to divine
the hidden and forgotten source,
who is transparent
where the moon drops out of the fog
to bathe,
but not to us

the retied heart
                where the wind glitters

for Ellen Tallman

a bird in the house

the truth flies   hungry, at least   and otherous,
of which — though it may be one — Kafka said troublingly,
it has many faces

                                        it's
the faces one wants, tripping the light shadows of   its
skin colours   of its wordy swiftness, angry and solvent,
of its loud remarks

                    as of feeding flocks   one
year, one, among the smallest birds in the Northwest, flew
into the house   a darting, panic thought   at the walls
and grasses   perched on the top right corner of the frame

of Tom Field's painting wherein adulterous Genji is found
out — so Lady Murasaki reads from her blue scroll — and
permitted me to take it in my hand   soft, intricate

mind   honouring   and lift it out into the air
and the next year, again, one flew into the house,
almost certain, like a visitor, gold-crowned   winged

floating about   odd discoveries   and alighted on the brim
of the lasagna dish   my hand trembled as I took it up
and moved slowly to lift it out of the window   into

the air   a kind of thinking   like everybody else
looking   for *a continuing contravention of limits and
of substance*

for Sharon Thesen

Muses, Dionysus, Eros

                      offerings to them can only be
all your life, old man

and I was boxing with a tough opponent   the footnote
says, 'Presumably Eros'   but I thought all three
in this otherness of home

and cowboyed it down Idaho way, east and west of Blaser, non-
populated, on the Portneuf River with railroads for horseback

and TV tells me St. Clare—whose poverty dreamed a transubstantiation
on the wall of her bedroom, God's problem—protects TV's
   deprivation,
and I asked St. Clare to help this kaleidoscope be asymmetrical, as the
world is in mind and heart

and, in a trance, pushed all 37 buttons to a brightout, having found
God's back with a little help from commercialism, and practical
Marxism, and implored as I craved, excessive and all ways

and a phone call of wishfulness came through just then   Stan sure
wished he could defend civilization this New Year   helplessly, I
promised to tape 80 years of Elliott Carter's intelligence, as soon as I
learned the *techne* of conversation, of fragments of *acellerandi* and
decellerandi—of violin, violin, viola, and cello answering one another,
worlding, until later, each instrument opposes, *laments, laughs,
ridicules and silences—both with and against* the possible beautiful year

and I was boxing with a tough opponent   the footnote
says, 'Probably Eros'

                                     reading Anacreon

Liveforever

'Where is Abraham buried?' you ask. Well, in the *Kabbalah*,
God has a terrible time getting Abraham to agree to die. In
the *Zohar,* where Abraham is initiate and David calls God by
the name 'Midnight,' the splendour is woven in the energies
of the Hebrew alphabet, a creation in language that is never
still. Now, looking at the three religions of Abraham — Hebrew,
Christian, and Muslim — I would say that Abraham, though
very much changed since 1700 BCE, is not dead. There's only
so much that a post-Catholic, polytheist exodic can say just
now.

for Samuel Truitt
August 1996

Image-Nation 26 (being-thus

'your path is poetry, your goal is beyond poetry,'
I once said, but don't hold me to it —
that was early one morning — a fragment
of waking up —
                        searching the presences
that weren't there — before the words carved them —

after crosswords with Sphinx and Chimera,
out of the watchwords of Basilisk, overheard
amidst the gallop of Unicorn's ivory hooves,
the blood in my veins carrying life back to
my heart —
                        I feel like flying, swimming, yelping,
bellowing, howling. I'd like to have wings,
a carapace, a rind, to breathe out smoke,
wave my trunk, twist my body, divide
myself up, to be inside everything, to drift
away with odours, develop as plans do,
flow like water, vibrate like sound, gleam
like light, to curl myself up into every
shape, to penetrate each stone, to get down
to the depth of matter — to be matter!   (Flaubert

a soul is there in the middle of its web,
touched by every *tug on its complicated structure—*
this continuous moment that is *poēsis—*
this not-not-being at the heart of this complicated
structure —
                        let us learn what rhythm holds us —   (Archilochus
our form —

64

one must assume that the human race is invisible
though still operatively present —   (Edwin Muir

our angel of our history — *His face is turned toward*
the past. Where we perceive a chain of events, he
sees one single catastrophe which keeps piling
wreckage and hurls it in front of his feet. The angel
would like to stay, awaken the dead,
and make whole what has been smashed.
But a storm is blowing from Paradise; it has
got caught in his wings with such violence
that the angel can no longer close them. This storm
insistently propels him into the future... while the debris
before him grows skyward.   (Benjamin

walking a rope at the end of our metaphysical journey,
tethered at *the extreme end of our metaphysical itinerary* — (Agamben

There is a goal, but no way; what we call the way is only
wavering —   (Kafka

...travelers in a train that has met with an accident in a tunnel,
and this place where the light of the beginning can no longer be seen,
and the light of the end is so very small a glimmer that the gaze
must continually search for it and is always losing it again, and
furthermore, it is not certain whether it is the beginning or the end
of the tunnel.   (Kafka

NOW-TIME   *JETZTZEIT*

Aitant, ses plus — inasmuch, no more, men and women live
as they live joyously —   (Sordello

in the original space that language loves, first heard
in the womb —

resoling and resewing for the goal, perhaps
we could begin again to imagine a *Purgatorio*
as a *continuous image of our poetic condition* —

(See Sollers

cutting the heart out to eat of it —
eating the heart out —

Seeing something simply in its being-thus — irreparable, but not
for that reason necessary; thus, but not for that reason contingent —
is love —   (Agamben

and of the being-beyond-itself —

            the strangest visitor last night when I went
            out for my last cigarette of the day — about
            the size of my thumb — attracted, rather
            helplessly, even drunkenly — yellow, black
            stripes, transparent wings — like a very large
            bee, two amazing red brushes on its head,
            striped with black, that seemed to feel for the
            light — or heat — it would fall, plop, wander,
            then fly up to the light — I've never seen a
            bug of such size in the air — seemed powerful
            and frightening, still helpless — gone
            this morning — I've searched for it, like
            happiness —

                        Written for Jery Zaslove.
            I've long noted the word love in his name.
                                1 October 2000

a true story of
I'm 19 — no, 20 —
looking for watercress
in the mind's ditches
cold, running ripple of strawberry
creek

    and Jack says
come on, let's go to the Trotskyite
meeting tonight —
            a fold of 14 there
and one stood up:
'I move we ban supernaturalist
religions'
        I elbowed Spicer and
said what if...
he said go for it
I stood up: 'Point of order.
I'm papal nuncio for the Bay Area.'
They kicked us out and changed
their meetings to a secret place.
Months later I ran into one of them.
I said how's it going, he said:
'Comes the Revolution, you'll hang
from a lamppost.' Unlikely as it may seem
his name was also Robin. A chill passed
over my joke —
now I'm 76 looking around for watercress.

6 July 2001

the Bible is as historical
as you or I
and feathered as our words
fly,
a crow there, a peacock,
a sparrow pecking sidewalk
crumbs.
We both know it takes centuries
to say that,
bumming it,
riding the rails of that railroad,
you and I whistling past
all stops.

8 August 2002

ROBERT MAJZELS
and ERÍN MOURE
(translators)

NICOLE BROSSARD

Notebook of Roses and Civilization

Over her four decades of writing and publishing poems and novels and essays — *textes* — Nicole Brossard has always shone an investigative light on every word that comes to her, and turned a demanding ear to each item of punctuation or notation. She sees the universe in the word for sand, and knows that it could be *sable mouvant*. So the translators of Nicole Brossard have to make poems we will love to read the way a carpenter loves a finished table. Majzels and Moure are not masters but divine servants of the English words they so carefully bring over to us. Inventive writers themselves, they are practiced translators who have here taken on a daunting project and succeeded beautifully.

Apparition of Objects

winter water blue melt backlit
life suddenly in thin chemise
steadfast
in questions and old silences

in the puzzle of proper nouns
and barking city: February
slow eyelashes that beckon to love
and spinning tops

foliage of word for word
gentleness that evades meaning
plunge into the dark
with metronome

crabs eels intestines
legs and antennae
destiny you said it
from memory
with a single verb

the thousand and one possibilities of the toe, the foot
the ankle
images in the subway glued to each other
faces pressed against the whys

the saliva the fingernails
it all goes beyond
adverbs and bones

the future the future
naked things design
audacity vertical

a woman in panties
half-spoken surrounded
by syntax and paintings

dark eyebrows
a starlet sings
an amphetamine clenched in her teeth

fire close to dying
at the edge of a forest
kiss that counts

someone standing
before an accident
of cars and fiction

under the eyelid:
time's measuring tape
dust in equilibrium

peoples and their signatures
their faces more alive
than crabs and pigeons in the shade
of cherry trees

poetry drawn back from daring
fiction if you ask me
hazelnut: image of an old
tomb with a squirrel

a photo repeated that sparks a taste
for pleasure with a grain of salt
on the tongue
a photo repeated
a stack of selves archived

big blue armchairs
their cloth arms worn down
by memory and odours
that intoxicate. Retina,
adjust your thoughts

emergency staircase on a slant
with slow blue flung at the sky
window and woman smiling

the rust the steel, broken panes
of America the colour of graffiti
then in slow motion: tulips appear
spinal cord
strange archives

on the iron rails
of a century the mud
of a day the immensity

Sombre: night flower
or calculated shadow
brief flame: hypothesis

Feinte speak reflection
seen through glasses
all words are ribbons

reading *lèvres* micro
i know the answer
poems that demand we open
the fire the heart: devour me

palace and ice
parentheses (duvet)
orange, epidermis
pillowcases
i beg of you: answer

birds pepper-coloured
a flight of silence with clouds
distant. I retrace my steps
touch here a woman's arm

tiny algae that enter
gastronomy
blue water imbued water
always another beginning

the lemon the martini the olive
all that amuses
then came night with its lampshades
describe the light
touch tomorrow

the immense everyday furled in the iris
a morning
of found orchids

DAVID W. McFADDEN

Why Are You So Sad?: Selected Poems
of David W. McFadden

David McFadden has been a major underground poet all his writing life, and the young poets discover him every year. He has always been the darling of the avant-garde, but he is the most readable poet on the planet. Like his hero William Blake, he lives at ease among the most supernatural of events, and gazes in wonderment at everyday things. As a poet he reminds you to be human, to be yourself in the world, and give it a chance to amaze you. While reading his beautiful, clear language, you sense that he is a trickster, but you cannot help believing every stanza he writes. If there is any such thing as an essential poet, here he is.

Margaret Hollingsworth's Typewriter

I was eating scrambled eggs in the Shamrock Restaurant
and the eggs tasted like Chinese food
so I said to the waitress I'm a person
who likes Chinese food but doesn't like
my eggs in the morning to taste like chicken fried rice
and she laughed and said it must have been
the green onions and suggested the next time
I come into the Shamrock for breakfast
I specify that I want Canadian green onions
with my scrambled eggs or I'll get Chinese again

and I said there won't be another time,
this is it, I'm a widely respected blah blah and blah
and well-regarded in the community too
and shouldn't have to subject myself
to such bad food. I'm finished, I said.
This used to be my favourite Irish-Chinese restaurant
in the entire West Kootenay
but this is it, I'm never coming back —
and through the kitchen door I could see
the Chinese chef covering his ears with his hands.

And so I went to pay my bill
and this is the really embarrassing part,
this is why I'm writing this poem
by hand, pencil on paper, because Margaret Hollingsworth's
typewriter has a three-prong plug
and all the outlets in the house are two-prongers
and her adapter is up at the college
and I begged her to let me cut the third prong off

so I could use her typewriter
because I had a simply overwhelming
desire to write this poem and she refused
and I told...oh, never mind all that.

This is the embarrassing part. After complaining
so vociferously about the eggs I went to pay my bill
and discovered I had no money with me
so I had to go home and get my wallet
and bring it back to the restaurant
making myself a liar for having said
this is it, I'm never coming back.
The waitress was very nice about it all.

Is it hard to write poetry?
Yes, I would say it is. For instance
in this poem I didn't know whether to start
by talking about the scrambled eggs
or the Smith Corona. And I didn't have
a lot of time to think about it
because I simply had to start the poem,
it was that urgent,
and then you have to torture yourself
wondering if it's all right to write about
writing in a poem and you keep resolving
never again to write about writing
and you always break your resolve.
It's as if writing has a will of its own
and wants to be written about
just like Margaret Hollingsworth's
typewriter.

My Body Was Eaten by Dogs

I met her while walking in Egypt
on the road to Oxyrhynchus
where the Ibycus papyrus was found.
Her body had been eaten by dogs,
torn into little pieces,
each piece
                        still glowing with life.

How I met her, I tripped on the road
then noticed the rock that caught my toe
was a face,
                        a large broken nose and a
                        once-smooth chin cracked and chipped.

She looked up at me with hardened eyes
silently pleading to be picked up

and I wondered what it would be like
to spend centuries without a workable body,
life clinging to small fragments of petrified flesh
like reflections to pieces of shattered glass.

And there she was lying like a rock
in the road, helpless, a living
rock among all the other rocks,
a living planet searching the heavens
for signs of life.

And finally as I hesitated wondering
if I had time to waste on this, this...

I mean it was a curious situation all right
but the landscape was loaded, overloaded
with equally curious situations
and I was in a hurry to reach the sea

and the strange black mouth opened
and I had a glimpse of the awful warmth
of a life that has nothing else
but warmth.

My body, she said,
was eaten by dogs.

And her mouth slowly closed again
like a clam with a morsel to digest
and she continued staring up at me
as if I were the first person
in five thousand years
to have noticed her lying on the road

and I picked her up
and put her in my bag
and eventually brought her back to Canada

and now she is sitting on my bookshelf
in my log cabin in Tuktoyaktuk
and every nine minutes or so
she opens her mouth to say
My body was eaten by dogs

and her shrunken blue-grey eyes
never close.

A Cup of Tea with Issa

I've never seen a raindrop fall on a frog's head but you have. You say the frog wiped away the water with his wrist and that's good enough for me.

Ever since I first heard it fifteen years ago your poem on the death of your son has been flitting in and out of my mind. And now I see there are two versions, the first having been revised on the later death of your daughter, in 1819, of smallpox. And now I want you to know that I hope you've been reunited with your sons and your daughters and your wives and your father, and that I prefer the first version.

The sun has dropped behind the mountains and the tiny cars on the long winding road way over on the other side of the lake have their lights on. And a sense of amazement springs up, amazement that we live in a world where the sun continually rises and sets.

The *Marasmius oreades* (delicious when fried with bacon) have formed a fairy ring in the shape of a giant number 3 in the courtyard lawn, reminding me of the time I saw three motorcycles parked diagonally at the curb in front of 111 Brucedale Avenue.

In October you can look at the sides of the mountains and see the patterns made by the deciduous trees which have become bright yellow or orange among the coniferous which have remained dark green. Sometimes it seems like a territorial war up there but the conflict between the two types of trees is probably more in my mind than on the slopes.

This morning the sky is blue but the tops of the mountains cling to thick giant puffs of pink and grey cloud. A small white cloud rises from the surface of the lake and tries to reach the big ones up above but by the time it gets halfway there it has almost completely disappeared.

It's pleasant to be so unhurried that you can see even the slowest-moving clouds moving. A part of me says I should be ashamed of myself but you know the more time you waste the more you get. It's like money.

On a rainy windy October morning a grey Volkswagen sits at the side of the road. It's covered with hundreds of small wet yellow leaves plastered on the trunk, on the hood, on the roof — in a strangely satisfying pattern. Was it the rain and the wind or was it a subtle and patient artist with a pot of glue? Of course it was the wind and the rain and of course it's a hackneyed idea. But for a moment I wonder. As you would have.

It's pleasant to have a cup of tea and think of you, Issa, and to think of others in the twentieth century having a cup of tea and thinking of you, Issa.

Last Chance to Hit Balls
(Six Tanka and Six Haiku)

I apologize
For getting mad at the guy
    Selling stale apples.
He said he watched me stalk off
Punching my head with my fist.

When I was sixteen
George Meyers said my hips were
    Shaped like a woman's.
I almost died. Now I wish
I'd bought a dress and makeup.

Reading *Kokoro*
In the noodle joint. Waitress
    Notices and smiles.
Says she found it too slow but
It's her mother's favourite book.

Sixteen peaches sit
Ripening slowly on the
    Branch of my window.

If I couldn't be
Me I'd like to be either
    John Wayne or my mom.

    Got a card from George —
He's in Capetown meeting with
    Batman, Superman,
And several other guys I
Met in Montevideo!

    Sometimes I think I
Invented the universe
    But that's silly, no?

    Whether or not we're
Sports-minded we all perhaps
    Have our own secret
Batting averages, win-loss
Records and sense of the crowd.

    I am a king who
Has three daughters, a daughter
    Who has three sisters.

That busboy knows his
Beeswax, at first I thought he
    Owned the bloody joint —
Next thing I know he's doing
Backflips up and down the bar.

There are wonderful
People in the world but I'm
    Not one, nor my friends.

Last chance to hit balls
For five hundred and twenty
    Miles. (Sign in *Tin Cup*.)

Slow Black Dog

Meditating in the back
of Jack's green Volkswagen
rolling along Highway 2
east of Paris

I'm conscious only of the motion
of things speeding against me
on both sides of my head,
eyes closed, and a sudden braking

and a breaking of that dream.
I'm in a moving car among green hills
and cow grazings of the world,
motels, gas stations of Ontario

and a dog slowly walking across
into our speeding lane, a black dog,
and in tall grass at roadside, a boy,
waving his arms, screaming.

The Big M

1. Every Sunday at noon during the summer the guy next door (Frank by name) treats his kids to a big watermelon. They mill about on the verandah and lawn eating big slices of it, and it is funny to hear, as the well-dressed devout file out of Garside Gospel Church ("Where the HOLY BIBLE is WHOLLY TAUGHT") half a block away, bells chiming, neat fussy Frank in a booming voice call out, "Be careful what you do with the seeds."

2. I'm in my cellar study
keeping cool

writing this poem quickly
because Joan is coming DOWN
with a KNIFE

and a cold
watermelon.

3. bpNichol hates watermelon.

ABOUT THE POETS
AND TRANSLATORS

JOHN ASHBERY was born in Rochester, New York, in 1927. He earned degrees from Harvard and Columbia, and he travelled as a Fulbright Scholar to France in 1955. Best known as a poet, he has published more than twenty collections, most recently *A Worldly Country* (Ecco, 2007). His *Self-Portrait in a Convex Mirror* (Viking, 1975) won the three major American prizes: the Pulitzer, the National Book Award, and the National Book Critics Circle Award. He has served as executive editor of *Art News* and as the art critic for *New York* magazine and *Newsweek*. A member of the American Academy of Arts and Letters and the American Academy of Arts and Sciences, he served as Chancellor of the Academy of American Poets from 1988 to 1999. The winner of many prizes and awards, both national and international, he has received two Guggenheim Fellowships and was a MacArthur Fellow from 1985 to 1990. His work has been translated into more than twenty languages. He lives in New York, and since 1990 he has been the Charles P. Stevenson Jr. Professor of Languages and Literature at Bard.

ROBIN BLASER is one of North America's most outstanding poets of the postwar period, having emerged from the Berkeley Renaissance of the 1940s and 1950s as a central figure in that burgeoning literary scene. He is professor emeritus at Simon Fraser University and has published several books of poems and numerous essays, many of which are included in *The Fire: Collected Essays of Robin Blaser* (University of California Press, 2006). In 2006, Blaser was the first poet to be honoured with The Griffin Trust for Excellence in Poetry's Lifetime Recognition Award.

NICOLE BROSSARD is a poet, novelist, and essayist who has published more than thirty books since 1965, including *These Our Mothers, Lovhers, Mauve Desert,* and *Baroque at Dawn.* She cofounded *La Barre du Jour* and *La Nouvelle Barre du Jour,* two important literary journals in Quebec. She has won two Governor General's Literary Awards for poetry, as well as le Prix Athanase-David, and her work has been translated into several languages.

ELAINE EQUI is the author of eleven books of poetry, including *The Cloud of Knowable Things* and *Voice-Over,* which won the San Francisco State Poetry Award. Her work has been widely anthologized and has appeared in publications such as *The New Yorker, American Poetry Review, The Best American Poetry* compilations, and *A Norton Anthology of Postmodern American Poetry.* She lives in New York with her husband, poet Jerome Sala, and teaches at New York University and in the MFA programs at The New School and City College.

CLAYTON ESHLEMAN is a professor emeritus of English at Eastern Michigan University. A poet and essayist, he was the founding editor of two of the most highly regarded literary magazines, *Caterpillar* and *Sulfur.* A recipient of the National Book Award and the Landon Translation Prize, he is the co-translator of *Aimé Césaire: The Collected Poetry* (University of California Press) and the author of *Juniper Fuse: Upper Paleolithic Imagination and the Construction of the Underworld.* Eshleman has also received a Guggenheim

Fellowship in Poetry, two fellowships from the National Endowment for the Arts, two fellowships from the National Endowment for the Humanities, and several research fellowships from Eastern Michigan University.

DAVID HARSENT was born in Devonshire. He has published nine collections of poetry, including *Legion*, which won the Forward Prize for best collection in 2005 and was shortlisted for both the Whitbread Award and the T. S. Eliot Prize, and *A Bird's Idea of Flight*, which was a Poetry Book Society Choice. He is a Fellow of the Royal Society of Literature, and in 2005 he was appointed Distinguished Writing Fellow at Sheffield Hallam University. He is currently working on a novel, *The Wormhole*, and a new collection of poems.

ROBERT MAJZELS is an award-winning novelist, playwright, poet, and translator. His most recent books are the novels *Apikoros Sleuth* and *The Humbugs Diet* (Mercury Press). He won the Governor General's Literary Award for Translation in 2000, and has translated, with Erín Moure, three books of poetry by Nicole Brossard, including *Notebook of Roses and Civilization*, which was shortlisted for the Governor General's Literary Award. He currently teaches creative writing at the University of Calgary.

DAVID W. McFADDEN has published over twenty books of poetry and prose, including *Gypsy Guitar*, nominated for a Governor General's Literary Award in 1987, and *The Art of Darkness*, nominated for a Governor General's Literary Award in 1984. He has recently published a travel book titled *An Innocent in Cuba* and a book of poetry called *Five Star Planet*. He lives in Toronto.

ERÍN MOURE is one of Canada's most eminent and respected poets, and a translator from French, Spanish, Galician, and Portuguese. Winner of the Governor General's Literary Award for *Furious*, the Pat Lowther Memorial Award for *Domestic Fuel*, and the A. M. Klein Poetry Prize for *Little Theatres* (which has also been published in Spain in Galician translation as *Teatriños*), Moure has published twelve books of poetry, including *A Frame of the Book*, co-published in the U.S. by Sun and Moon Press, and five books of poetry in translation, including *Sheep's Vigil by a Fervent Person* by Fernando Pessoa, shortlisted for the 2002 Griffin Poetry Prize and the 2002 City of Toronto Book Prize. Moure lives in Montreal.

CÉSAR VALLEJO (1892–1938) was born in Santiago de Chuco, a small town in the Andean sierra of northern Peru. His 1922 book-length sequence, *Trilce*, was one of only two collections of his poetry to be published during his lifetime, the other being *Los heraldos negros* (*The Black Heralds*). Vallejo was a political radical and a communist, and for part of his life lived in exile in Paris, where he met Antonin Artaud, Pablo Picasso, and Jean Cocteau. Vallejo wrote stories, essays, a novel, and several plays, and is considered one of the great poetic innovators of the twentieth century.

ACKNOWLEDGEMENTS

The publisher thanks the following for their kind permission to reprint the work contained in this volume:

"Someone You Have Seen Before," "Token Resistance," "Chapter 11, Book 35," "Memories of Imperialism," "The New Higher," and "Interesting People of Newfoundland" from *Notes from the Air: Selected Later Poems* by John Ashbery are reprinted by permission of Ecco, an imprint of HarperCollins Publishers.

"Luck Unluck One Luck," "Suddenly," "a bird in the house," "Muses, Dionysus, Eros," "Liveforever," "Image-Nation 26 (being-thus," "a true story of," and "the Bible is as historical" from *The Holy Forest: Collected Poems of Robin Blaser* are reprinted by permission of University of California Press.

"Apparition of Objects" from *Notebook of Roses and Civilization* by Nicole Brossard, translated by Robert Majzels and Erín Moure, is reprinted by permission of Coach House Books.

"Invocation," "John Coltrane's Central Park West," "Found in Translation," "Echo," "I Interview Elaine Equi on the Four Elements," "Prescription," "Sometimes I Get Distracted," "The Banal," and "Dolor" from *Ripple Effect: New and Selected Poems* by Elaine Equi are reprinted by permission of Coffee House Press.